F E G

Ridiculous ~~Stupid~~ **Poems for Intelligent Children**

POEMS

by **Robin Hirsch**

WITH THE ASSISTANCE OF

Benjamin Joshua Jaglom Hirsch

AND A CRITICAL INTRODUCTION BY

Alexander Max Jaglom Hirsch

Illustrated by Ha

Megan Tingley Books

LITTLE, BROWN AND COMPANY

New York ∽ An AOL Time Warner Company

To Bjørn Ottøbë
—R. H.

To Devin and Danny
—Ha

Text copyright © 2002 by Robin Hirsch
Illustrations copyright © 2002 by Ha

First Edition

Library of Congress Cataloging-in-Publication Data

Hirsch, Robin.
FEG : stupid (ridiculous) poems for intelligent children/ by Robin Hirsch ; with the assistance of Benjamin Joshua Jaglom Hirsch and a critical introduction by Alexander Max Jaglom Hirsch ; illustrated by Ha — 1st ed.
    p. cm.
    ISBN 0-316-36344-8
1. Children's poetry, English. 2. Play on words — Juvenile literature. [1. English poetry. 2. Play on words.] I. Title: FEG. II. Title: Stupid (ridiculous) poems for intelligent children. III. Ha, ill. IV. Title.

PR6058.I55 F2 2002
821.914 — dc21   00-064965

10 9 8 7 6 5 4 3 2

TWP

Printed in Singapore

The illustrations for this book were done in Adobe Illustrator.
The text was set in Triplex Regular and Bold.

CONTENTS

CRITICAL INTRODUCTION

Be where?
What shout?
Take air!

These poems are stupid.

Some of these poems are really stupid.*

Signed,
Your friend,

Alexander Max Jaglom Hirsch
(a.k.a. Sasha)

---

*Except for about three lines that I helped write.

4

BROTHERLY REBUTTAL

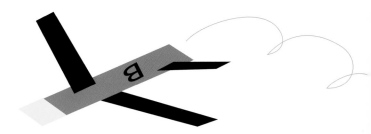

I discountenance, disavow, and thoroughly disparage
dese remarks.

These poems are *not* stupid. They may be ridiculous, but
they are *not* stupid.*

Signed,
Your other friend,

Benjamin Joshua Jaglom Hirsch
(a.k.a. Benjy)

---

*Except, maybe, for the one or two lines my brother helped write.

HOW YOU CAME INTO THE PICTURE

These poems are all the result of fooling around. Three of us (one older person and two considerably younger ones) developed the habit of tossing words around when we ran out of **footballs** (or when we weren't allowed to use them), at home, in the car, at the beach, in restaurants, wherever we happened to be. Sometimes we would make dreadful **puns.** Sometimes we'd **laugh hysterically.** Sometimes we'd **groan.** And sometimes we'd sit at the kitchen table and put some of our nonsense down on paper and arrange it into **poems.**

Then one day we showed some of these poems to our friend Julia, whose sons are pretty much the same age as two of us. And she showed them to Megan Tingley at Little, Brown, and **Megan (a gem)** — sorry, we couldn't resist, it's a **palindrome** — because she's an editor and wields enormous power, realized she could show them to a lot more people. Which is how you come in.

WILD GOOSE CHASE

We hope that you can enter these poems with the same spirit of play in which we wrote them. And that once you catch the ball you might decide to throw it around on your own — with friends, relatives, teachers, pets (well, maybe not pets). Some of these poems are **puzzles,** some are **games,** some might send you off on a **wild goose chase.**

Now, a wild goose is a very hard thing to catch (much harder than a football) and not much use when you do. So most normal people think a wild goose chase is a waste of time. We, however, love them. We call them **WGCs,** and we go on them all the time. You know why? Because we like to follow things, not to their logical conclusion (which may be great in math class), but wherever they may lead. We are more interested in the trip than in the destination. The great adventure writer Robert Louis Stevenson probably put it best. He said, "To travel hopefully is better than to arrive." Sure beats, "Are we there yet?"

PROVISIONS

Now, on any trip it's a good idea to take along provisions. On a normal trip you might have a **candy bar** or a **sandwich** or a Thermos of **nice hot soup.** But this is a wild goose chase and it involves language, perhaps the wildest WGC of all. So you'll need very different provisions. You're going to be a hunter or, perhaps better, a **detective.** There are likely to be **clues** to follow, or scents (or, more likely, given who we are, non-scents). You may start with a word, or even a letter, and want to track it through all kinds of undergrowth or overgrowth or thickets (or even thinnets, for that matter). So instead of a candy bar, may we suggest . . . a **dictionary**?

DETECTIVE STORY

But why just one dictionary? Why not two or three or eight? Probably, somewhere, lying around the house, you have a decent, standard dictionary. But how about a dictionary of **slang**? And a dictionary of **quotations**? And a **thesaurus**? And the grandfather of all modern dictionaries, the *Oxford English Dictionary* (all ten volumes, not to mention the supplement)? And since our language has its roots in Greek and Latin and Anglo-Saxon, and got invaded and changed over time by French and German and Spanish and Italian and Yiddish and . . . well, you get the idea.

Now, this isn't just the standard publisher's ploy of trying to sell you more books (although, to be truthful, they'd be delighted). It's just that, as a detective, it's useful to see what other detectives who've already visited **the scene of the crime** have figured out, and who agrees with whom, and who's tampered with **the evidence,** and how things have changed over time, and, most importantly, what *you,* **the detective in charge** right now, can figure out.

ANCILLARY PARAPHERNALIA

The American poet Archibald MacLeish wrote:

> A poem should not mean
> But be

We only half agree. Half the fun of poetry is figuring out what the author meant, or what he thought he meant, or — the most fun of all — what he meant but didn't know he meant. If you look at an annotated edition of *Hamlet,* for example, you'll find generations of readers arguing with each other across the centuries over what Shakespeare really meant. It's a kind of literary **time travel.** Or **archaeology.** Or **chat room.** You can travel back or dig down all the way to that moment where Shakespeare first put quill to parchment — and join the conversation.

To this end, we've supplied you with all sorts of **ancillary paraphernalia** — which is just a fancy way of saying "other stuff." You'll find **introductions, rebuttals, footnotes,** an **envoi,** even a **glossary,** in which you can look up words like *glossary.* Most poets have to wait until they're dead before they get this kind of treatment.

So, don't be shy. Jump in. Argue back. Join the conversation.

F*E*G

Abie's seedy effigy
Eight chide Jake: a lemon
O peek:
You are as tea
You feed double
You axe why
See?
. . . Horsehead!

This poem looks like **gibberish,** right? (Nice word, by the way, *gibberish*. . . .) You might want to try reading it out loud — a good thing to do with all poems. Unfortunately, it will still be gibberish, but it may fall into some instantly recognizable pattern. **Ping!** A bell will go off. Then there are only two other things to worry about: **Horsehead** (you may need to hire a British detective to get to the bottom of this one); and the title of the poem — and the book itself — **FEG.** We've searched high and low, in every dictionary we could lay our hands on, and we haven't been able to find *feg.* But there must be a reason we used it, right?

Now, if you wanted to be really adventurous, could you, if you had to, by whatever stretch of your imagination, make sense of this nonsense?

YOU ENTER A POEM . . .

You enter a poem
Just like you enter a room.
You open the door
And what do you see?
A sink, for example,
A bathtub, a toilet
(Does a toilet belong in a poem?)
And you say to yourself, "Aha!
It's a bathroom."

The next time you enter
You know it's a bathroom
And you notice
The towels on the rack
And their color
The mirror, the tiles, the sofa
(What? There's a sofa? In the bathroom?)
And you say: "Aha!
It's that kind of a bathroom."

It was bedtime. We were reading a poem by Frank O'Hara called "A True Account of Talking to the Sun at Fire Island." It's a favorite of ours, partly because we have a little beach house on Fire Island, but it's not exactly easy to follow. We had read it dozens of times. We still didn't have any easy answers. We went into the bathroom to brush our various teeth. Benjy said, "I don't understand. Every time we read

The third time you enter
You realize
One of the towels is frayed
There are streaks on the mirror
And the person who did the grouting
Messed up in that corner.
You open the drawers and the cabinets
You empty them
You take an inventory:
Toothbrushes, toothpaste, cotton balls, cleanser,
Toilet paper
(Does toilet paper belong in a poem?)
Not to mention
The childproof bottles of pills —
Which you know of course how to open —
And you say to yourself: "Aha!
It's that kind of a
This is how you enter a
I'm beginning to know this
Poem."

---

it, we see different things." **Aha!** Never be afraid to say you don't understand. Sometimes not under-
standing is the beginning of wisdom.

This is how "You Enter a Poem . . ." came into being. It goes to show that anything — even something you don't quite understand — can be an inspiration; any place — no matter how humble — can
be a setting; and all sorts of everyday objects — no matter how prosaic — can be the stuff of poetry.

Do you have a **nickname**? Very often, like Ed for Edward in this poem, it's a diminutive (an affectionate shortening) of your real name. Alexander, who wrote the critical introduction to this book, is referred to in this house as Sasha, which is the Russian diminutive for Alexander. Actually, the Russians are — if you'll pardon the **oxymoron** — big on diminutives, so by some of his Russian relatives he is sometimes called Sashinka, which is a diminutive of a diminutive. By the way, the word *nickname* itself is a bit of a mystery, requiring further detective work. We know that *nick* means *cut* or *notch*. It's also short for Nicholas — but that would imply that there is only one true Nick name. Which is clearly not the case, and which brings us to:

On the fritz — Fritz is a German nickname, or, more accurately, a diminutive for the name Friedrich. In the early part of the 20th century it was used as an informal name for all Germans (so, incidentally, were **Jerry, Hans,** & **Heinie,** short for Heinrich— and your bottom). We try not to do that sort of thing anymore, but in the early part of the 20th century such **monikers** were used more innocently. Before

BE*LAT*ED*LY

Edward Lee's alarm clock
Is always on the fritz
He lays it out upon the floor
In many different bits.
It drives his wife bananas
For everywhere she treads
Are nuts and bolts and widgets
Underfoot and under beds.
She wakes him in the morning
By banging on his head
And tweaking his proboscis
Until he's out of bed.
And then she yells
She yells and moans
She yells repeatedly,
"Get out of bed, you lazybones
And don't BE LATE, ED LEE!"

World War I all sorts of cheap stuff was imported from Germany and when, as happens with cheap stuff, things broke down, they were said to be, you guessed it, not on the Jerry, Hans, or Heinie, but *on the . . .*

Bananas — We haven't found a satisfactory explanation for why this particular fruit is used to mean *crazy.* But then, why *nuts?* And, furthermore, why *nutty as a fruitcake?*

Widgets are gadgets, usually ones that are unnecessary or useless or that don't work. In the 1920s in the New York garment industry, widgets were ornamental trimmings or frills added to clothing. Which meaning came first, the inquiring **wordsleuth** might wonder. . . .

Proboscis — One of those wonderful words that come from the Greek (*pro,* meaning *before* or *in front of,* and *boskein,* meaning *to feed* or *graze*). It's used to refer to an elephant's trunk, or by some of us, when we're being naughty, to someone's nose; usually the *sc* is pronounced as though it were just *s* but we, harking back to the Greek, like to pronounce it *sk.* We think it sounds better. What do you think?

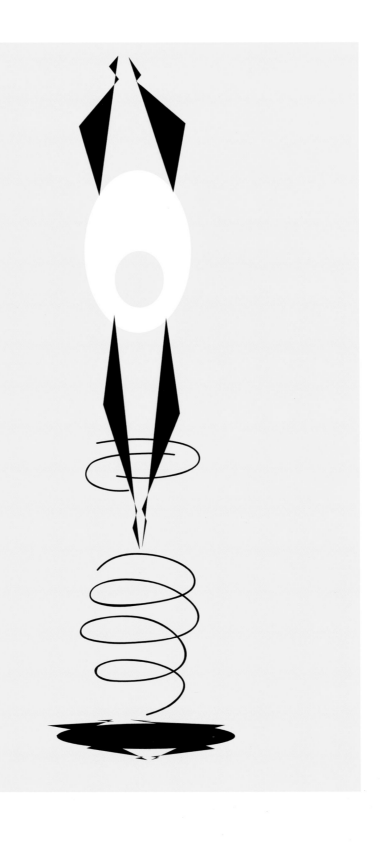

LEV*I*TATE

Sergei Diaghilev got up for breakfast
And discovered an egg on his plate
Not any old egg
A dancing egg
An egg that jumped out of its crate
He watched that egg in astonishment
He watched it jump and fly
He watched it perform a pirouette
Halfway up to the sky
And then, oy vay,
I'm sad to say,
I'm sorry to relate,
That dancing egg,
That rotten egg
Jumped off its plate
And the late
Great
Sergei Diaghi
LEV*IT*ATE

Sergei Pavlovich Diaghilev (1872 — 1929), perhaps the greatest of all ballet producers, was the founder of the Ballets Russes.

Oy vay — You won't find this in most English dictionaries, let alone Shakespeare. It's Yiddish, the great vernacular language of the Jews of Eastern Europe. Some Yiddish words/phrases — **meshuggeh, chutzpah, oy vay** — have entered at least conversational English through the great migrations of Jews from Eastern Europe in the late 19th century and the ministrations of some of their children who became comedians — the Marx Brothers, Sid Caesar, Danny Kaye, Mel Brooks, etc. The standard guide to Yiddish is Leo Rosten's wonderful *The Joys of Yiddish* — add that to your dictionary list. *Oy vay* is actually short for *Oy vay is mir,* which translates quite literally as *O woe is me.* Perhaps Shakespeare did know Yiddish after all. . . .

HIGH COOL

A super seven-
teen syllable Japanese
Air conditioner

There are many poetic forms — **sonnet, villanelle, limerick, clerihew.** . . . This is not one of them. It is, however, O great investigator, a formal **haiku.** (So, by the way, is the previous sentence.)

In Japan, where this form originated, it is strictly limited to seventeen syllables, arranged in three lines (5+ 7+ 5 = 17), and a seasonal topic. Poets in English have begun to experiment outside these limitations (see, for example, *The Haiku Anthology,* edited by Cor van den Heuvel, or the innumerable Internet sites devoted to haiku). Not us, however — we're strictly formal.

You might want to try your own hand at haiku — as formal or informal as you like. Haiku is, or are (haiku, remember, just like fish, is singular, and also plural — **whoops,** another haiku!), like throwing stones into a pond. You make a little splash, but if you're successful, the ripples keep going, not just in your pond, but in your mind — and more importantly, in ours.

> Haiku, like stones thrown
> into a pond, make ripples
> and reverberate.

For goodness' sake, stop, before you turn the whole world into this drivel. (**Oh, no,** not again. . . .)

EYE RHYME

Underneath a shady bough
I'm startled by a sudden cough
I fear that someone wants my dough
And figure that I've had enough

Rhyme is generally defined by *sound.* Words are said to rhyme when one or more syllables (usually at the end of the word) have the same sound, regardless of how they're spelled. For example, **word, heard, bird, curd, nerd, purred, stirred** are all spelled differently, but they all rhyme. The point of reading most poems aloud is the satisfaction of hearing such sounds repeating, of anticipating them, of waiting for them to fall into place like a bar on a stable door. (We dedicate this simile to our lovely editor, **Meganagem,** who wanted us to elaborate on figures of speech.) You could call all conventional rhyme **ear rhyme.**

Eye Rhyme is the exact opposite. Here, everything *looks* the same but *sounds* different. So it rhymes, not to the ear but to the eye — hence eye rhyme. It also makes absolutely no sense to read it aloud — since you only get it by looking at it. We thought of two other similar spellings with different sounds — **hiccough** and **through.** One we abandoned — *hiccough* is now usually spelled *hiccup*. The other we through into the next poem.

EWE RHYME

There once was a man whose name was Lou
Whose favorite dish was lamb ragout
He liked nothing better than a stew
Thickened with a tasty roux

On one side of him lived farmer Hugh
Who had a lovely lamb or ewe
He watched her grow up straight and true
He loved that lambkin through and through

On the other side lived farmer Stu
Whose cows would ruminate and moo
At milking time they'd form a queue
And frolic in the mud or boue

Lou licked his lips and muttered, "Ooh!"
"Aha!" he thought, "I'll score a coup.
I need one thing each from those other two."
And he knew exactly what to do.

We made up "Ewe Rhyme" as a companion for "Eye Rhyme." We managed to come up with 21 different ways of spelling the same sound. If you can think of any more, we'd love to hear from yewe. . . .

There are many words in this poem that come from the French. Some of them — **ragout, roux** — are cooking terms (the basis for all classical Western cooking — or *cuisine*, to use another French word — is French). Others — like **queue, coup, adieu** — are straightforward French words used quite matter-of-factly in English. And then there's **boue**, which means *mud*, but which usually appears in English only in the context of one glorious phrase — *nostalgie de la boue*, literally *nostalgia for the mud*. You may be a little young to get the full import of this (the expression *slumming* comes closest, though nowhere near close enough), but it's a great phrase to pull out nonchalantly at the dinner table, as in, "What's wrong, Daddy, are you suffering from *nostalgie de la boue* . . . or is it just plain old *Weltschmerz?*"

He bade his loving wife adieu,
Grabbed his son, Zbigniew,
Claude and Mario Lemieux,
The Shipping News by Annie Proulx,
And paddled off in his old canoe.

The boat was carved from seasoned yew
He left in search of milk and ewe
Now if he could just have taken you
And UN Secretary U
He would, with quite considerable hue,
Have slowly hove back into view
Bearing yew, ewe, you, and U.
      But he didn't.

Zbigniew — Zbigniew is a Polish first name. In Polish it's pronounced as though the last letter were a *v*. We've Americanized it here, partly in honor of President Carter's National Security Adviser, Zbigniew Brzezinski, neither of whose names we can pronounce properly.

Claude and Mario Lemieux — One (or, depending on who's counting, two) of the great contributions of Alexander Max Jaglom Hirsch, a.k.a. Sasha, a.k.a. Sashinka, who lives for hockey.

Annie Proulx won the Pulitzer Prize for her great novel, *The Shipping News*. We happened to be at the same birthday party in Vermont some years ago and the four of us wound up playing the bongos together. It's important, if you intend to become a writer, to have something reliable to fall back on, like bongo playing.

UN Secretary U — We have taken a little liberty here. The United Nations is presided over by a Secretary General. One of the great things about the UN is that the Secretary General, arguably the most influential international figure in the world, has generally come from one of the smallest, least influential countries, like Sweden, Egypt, Peru, Ghana, or in the case of U Thant, Burma (which is now called Myanmar). We wouldn't dream of calling him U (or even **Hey U**) in person — only in a poem.

Hue in this context is usually part of the phrase *hue and cry* — otherwise it means *tint*. But since *hue* and *cry* mean essentially the same thing, we've dispensed with *cry* and allowed ourselves what is called in the trade poetic license. Poetic license is one of the great excuses —try it at school someday.

CATO

O Cat,
Cato
Ate your taco
Now he wants your coat
And a cot to lie in —
Act, O noble feline!

We like titles. Sometimes titles take as much thought and tinkering as the poem itself. Our original title was a lot longer than the present one; indeed it was a lot longer and more complicated than the poem. But **Meganagem** thought it was too much. Anyhow, since footnotes are for arguing back (even to your editor), here it is:

CHRISTOPHER SMART

APOSTROPHIZES

HIS CAT, JEOFFRY,

AND EXHORTS HIM TO DEFEND HIMSELF

AGAINST THE DEPREDATIONS OF

A FAMOUS ROMAN STATESMAN

What do you think? Maybe you need a little more information?

Christopher Smart was a well-known 18th-century poet and lunatic — he ended up bankrupt in an asylum, a terrible warning to all poets. He also possessed one of the most famous cats in English poetry, **Jeoffry,** rivaled only by T. S. Eliot's collection of cats (in *Old Possum's Book of Practical Cats*), whom Andrew Lloyd Webber made internationally famous in his musical called (eponymously) *Cats.* . . .

There are some nice, juicy, long words in this title, which we thought lent a suitably high-flown tone to what is after all a tiny poem. You might want to check one of your now-numerous dictionaries and see whether **apostrophe,** which comes from the Greek, can mean something other than a punctuation mark. And as for **exhort** and **depredation,** they come from the Latin, which is entirely appropriate given the new (eponymous) hero of this poem, who is . . .

Ah, yes, as you have doubtless figured out, sublime detective, the famous Roman statesman is **Cato.** Actually, there were two of him: **Cato the Elder,** who was called the Censor, because he tried to reform the morals of his fellow-citizens, and his great-grandson, **Cato the Younger,** who, amongst other distinguished acts, committed suicide (a very noble Roman thing to do). Take your pick.

All clear? Now, by comparison, isn't the poem incredibly simple? It's just the same four letters rearranged in each line to make a new word or words. You can do it in a jiffy with other words.

The real trick is getting the title.

MURDER MOST VOWEL

When pirates sailed the Spanish main
They wore a fierce and savage mien
Much more fierce than yours or mine
The wind would howl and rage and moan
And they'd sail off beneath the moon —
  And you'd be dead.

If you were to have only one book in your life, it should probably be the *Collected Works of Shakespeare*. And if you were to read only one play of Shakespeare's, it should probably be *Hamlet*. *Hamlet* is the most quoted — and misquoted — play ever written. Check it out for yourself — *Hamlet*, Act I, Scene v— and see whether our title is a quotation or a misquotation. Of course, if it's a misquotation, it's a deliberate misquotation. . . .

You can commit your own (linguistic) murder by taking any one-syllable word and seeing whether it will survive a change through all the vowel sounds (or at least, the obvious ones) — e.g., **Nate, neat, night, note, newt;** and even some of the minor variations — **gnat, net, nit, not, nut;** and so on. Finally, if you're really adventurous, see if you can write a poem (and, of course, a title).

A PALINDROME
IS NOT
A PALINDROME

Some people have friends around the corner
Some have friends next door
Some have friends in Bangor, Maine
Some have friends in Bangalore

Some people have friends in foreign countries
Some have friends at home
But I've got a pal who comes and goes
    who backs and forths
    who to's and fro's
I've got a PAL*IN*DROME

Gertrude Stein, one of America's great gifts to eccentricity and language, famously wrote, "A rose is a rose is a rose." In this regard (and it really is only in this regard) she resembles Mozart, who once, after playing a new piano sonata, was asked what it meant. He promptly sat down and played it again. Sort of reminds you of Archibald, doesn't it? (Doesn't mean, but is . . . ?)

    In art, as in nature, certain things just are. However, there are occasions when something just isn't, and this is one of them.

BUT NOT NOW
A
WONTON TUB

I walked into a Chinese restaurant,
The waiter said to me,
"Would you like a giant bowl of wontons
Or do you have to pee?"
I said to the waiter,
"I can't believe you know —
I love your famous wontons
But I've really got to go.
So, first things first,
I love your grub
But not now a wonton tub."

There are great palindromes — **A man, a plan, a canal — Panama** comes to mind. There are enormously complex palindromes — the experimental 20th-century French writer Georges Perec is reputed to have composed a 5,000-letter palindrome, but then he also wrote an entire novel without using the letter *e* (the most common letter in the language) and then topped himself by writing an entire novel where the *only* vowel he used was the letter *e* — try writing even one halfway decent sentence using *e* as your only vowel.

This, on the other hand, may well be the lamest, most pathetic palindrome ever composed. Actually, the poem was written (or rather made up spontaneously) in the car to try and justify the pitiful palindrome that comes at the end. Surely, you can do better.

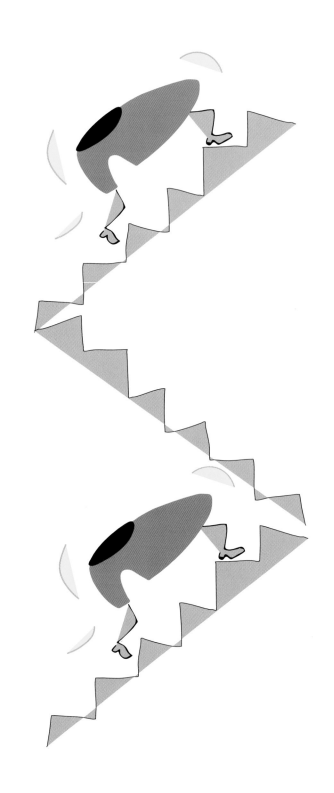

ON*O*MAT*O*POE*IA

Her mother always told her
When she came in the door,
"Take your shoes off, Pia,
Don't wipe them on the floor."
But Pia never listened
She tromped right up the stair
She took her shoes to bed with her
She didn't have a care.
Finally her mother
Could not stand it anymore
She raced up to the bedroom
And let out a mighty roar:
"My dearest darling daughter,
Remove those shoes, you hear,
Take them down into the hall
And put them ON A MAT, O PIA!"

Another one of those seemingly unpronounceable (and unspellable) words that come from the Greek —
in this case, from *onoma*, which means *name*, and *poiein*, which means *create* or *make*. From *poiein*,
by the way (and her relatives, *poietes* and *poiema*), we also get *poet*, *poetry*, and *poem*, literally a
maker (of verses), or an arrangement (of words).

Anyhow, **onomatopoeia** means to make words that imitate the sound of the named object, for
example, *roar* and *tromp* in this **poiema** and the operative word in the next poem. . . .

It was summer. We had put new doors into our beach house (on Fire Island, remember?). Unfortunately they wouldn't open all the way. What's the word for that, Benjy wanted to know. **Flush.** You mean, as in poker? **Yup.** Does it mean anything else? Sure does.

If words with different meanings are spelled the same way, they are called **homographs** (from the Greek again — *homos,* meaning *the same;* and *graphein,* meaning *to write*). So *bow,* as in bow and arrow, and *bow,* as in the bow of a ship, are homographs: they are spelled the same way, but they mean different things, have different origins, and are pronounced differently. They are the same words to the eye, but not to the ear (sound familiar?).

This is not the same thing as a **homophone,** which means literally *having the same sound.* So *bow,* as in bow of a ship, and *bough,* as in bough of a tree, are pronounced the same but have pro-

FLUSH

Feeling suddenly unusually rich

(flush)

I threw open the door until it lay
    flat against the wall

(flush)

There on the ground lay
    five cards of the same suit

(flush)

Boy, was my face
    the color of a heart or diamond

(flush)

I ran into the bathroom
    and threw them down the toilet
    (does a toilet belong in a poem?)

FLUSH!

nouncedly different meanings (and spellings). They are the same words to the ear, but not to the eye.

Now, just to make things more interesting, **flush** is neither a graph nor a phone, it's a *nym* — a **homonym,** which means *having the same name.* In other words, in all its multiple meanings, it has the same spelling *and* the same pronunciation. So it appears to be the same word both to the eye *and* to the ear. Out of context, even the brain has a hard time figuring it out — you need a context to flush out the meaning **(whoops, sorry!).** In the case of **flush,** most of the meanings (and there are more) can be traced to a common root in Flemish, French, and Spanish, having to do with **fullness** and **flow** — the fullness of the wallet or of the hand (in poker), the rush of blood to the face or of water to the toilet, and so on. Now, how did those doors get to be so **rich** and **red?**

Many words have multiple personalities. It's nothing to be ashamed of.

DE*LI*CIOUS

A* licious
B* licious
C* licious
D*
   lightful

We fought tooth and nail to keep this poem in so our **illustrious illustrator** would have some room for his art.

COUNTING TO INFINITY

I love you   1 ever

2 ever

3 ever

4 ever

more

It is of course impossible to count to infinity. That's what the mathematicians tell us. But if you're a **philologist** (a lover of language — from the Greek again: *philos*, meaning *love*, and *logos*, meaning *word*) you can beat the mathematicians at their own game.

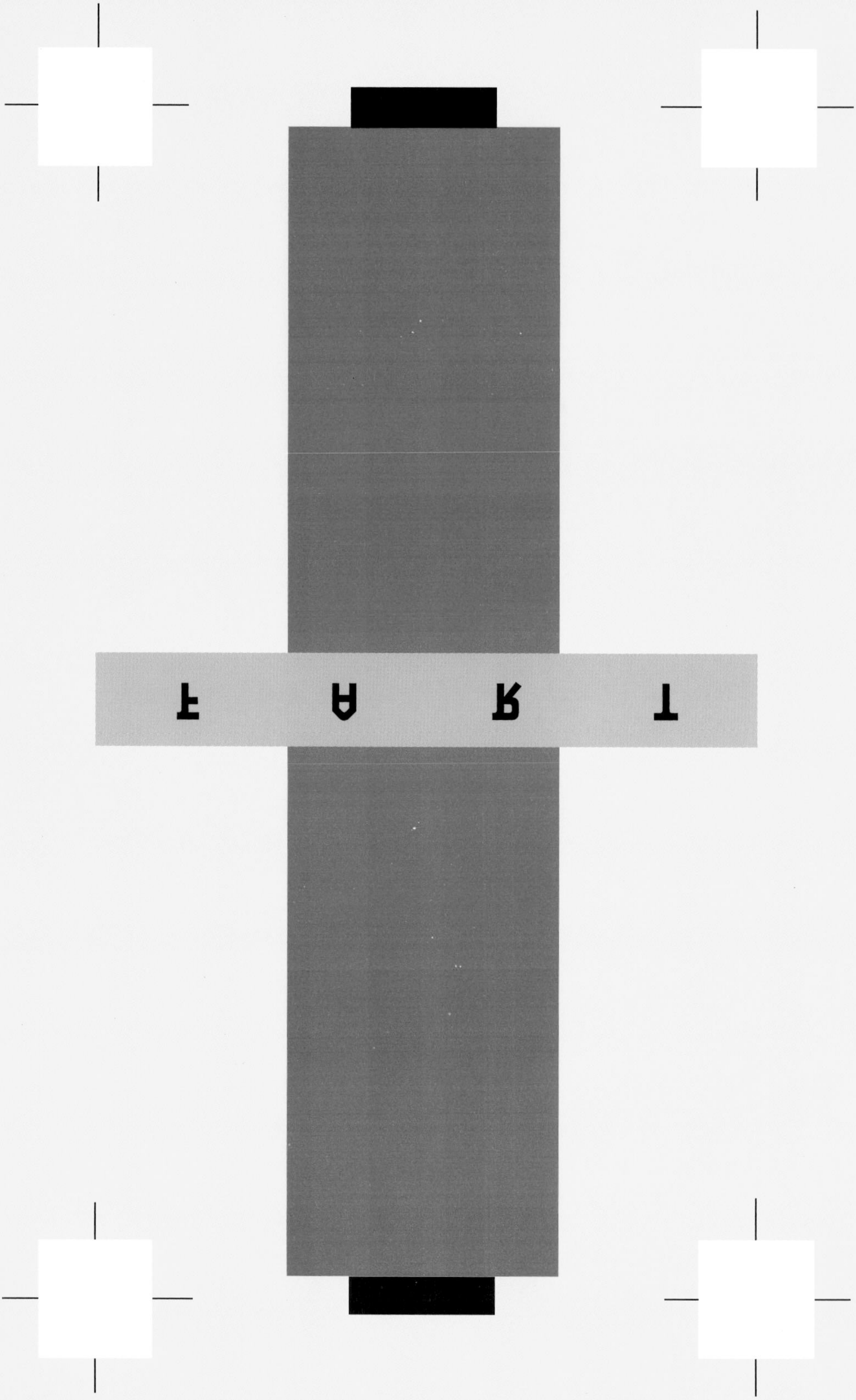
P A R T

DR. SPOONER WRITES THE MENU

To begin:
Marinated parts of harm.
And then, if lunch,
A chilled grease sandwich,
Or, if dinner,
Brightly leaded chalk pops.
And to drink:
A nice hot mug of hose rip tea
Or a nice bold class of gear.
And for dessert
May we suggest
Our truly delicious
Fresh true fart.

The Reverend William A. Spooner (1844 — 1930), Warden of New College, Oxford, was famous for unintentionally transposing the first letters of words in the same sentence. For example, he told one student he was going into town on a "well-boiled icicle," and another, who was flunking: "Sir, you have tasted a whole worm. You have hissed my mystery lectures. You were fighting a liar in the quadrangle. You will leave Oxford by the town drain." (Oxford and Cambridge are always up, even if you're coming from, say, Manchester, which is in the North, and conversely, everything else, including London, which is in the South but rather larger, is of course down — which tells you what Oxford and Cambridge think of the rest of the world, and, incidentally, which train to catch).

   We were sitting in a café at the beach, looking at the menu, when, lo and behold, GRILLED CHEESE SANDWICH transmogrified itself before our eyes, and the rest was just a matter of frying to Tigger out tot to wheat.

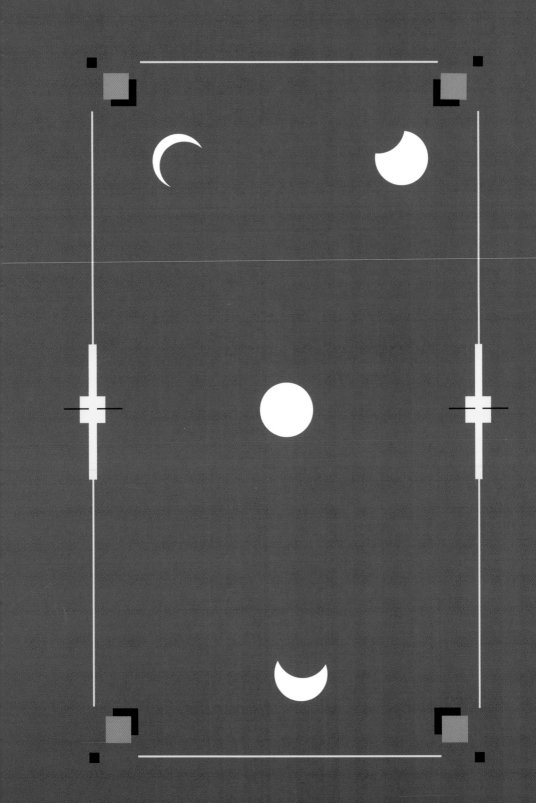

SONNET

S ON . . . I do love thee more than any starre

O r moon or planet or yon Milkie Waye

N ay, thou art more precious than a Snickers Barre:

N ot Mars itself can dim thy glorious raye.

E ach morning, though that other sunne doth rise

T o herald the arrival of new daye,

F ull dawn comes onlie when thy Choc'late eyes

O pen t'invite the waking world to play.

R owntree, Nestlé, Hershey, all these planets fly,

M oved by thy Baby Ruth, thy Lorna Doone.

Y ou are the Candie Apple of mine eye:

S on, thou art my sun, I thy revolving moon —

O rbiting around thee I shall never fret

N ow I have caught thee in my loving . . . NET.

A **sonnet** is a fourteen-line poem, and is perhaps the best-known poetic form in the Western world (in contrast to our beloved haiku, which comes from the East). Generally the first eight lines state a theme or an idea, which is resolved in some way in the last six lines (particularly in the last two, which form a rhyming couplet). There is a formal rhyme scheme, which in traditional English examples is generally *abab, cdcd, efef, gg*. We are, of course, nothing if not formal.

The word *sonnet* comes from the Italian *sonetto*, meaning *a little sound* or *song*. This is probably because the first great practitioner of the sonnet *was* Italian — the great 14th-century poet and humanist Petrarch (his real name was Francesco Petrarca); he wrote a whole series of sonnets to his beloved Laura, who was unfortunately married to someone else at the time.

If you're writing in English, your great inspiration (certainly, ours) is going to be Shakespeare, who wrote CLIV of the greatest *sonetti* in the English language.

You might also want to check out what an **acrostic** is. Sasha will tell you it's something you play lacrosse with.

CHA*RIS*MA

In New York there's always an alarm going off
And a garbage truck gurgitating
And a pesky dog barking
And that astonishing phenomenon known to its denizens
As alternate side of the street parking.
Basically it means
That the first thing you do in the morning
Tired and yawning
Is go out and move your car
From one side of the street to the other —
Unless you're my mother
Who can never remember
Where she left it the night before —
Three blocks away or outside the front door?

Charisma is (surprise, surprise) another Greek word, pretty much taken wholesale into English. In Greek, *karis* means *grace, beauty, kindness.* Christianity took it to mean a specific kind of grace or gift or talent, particularly for prophecy. In general (and here we move from religion into politics) it has come to denote a special quality of leadership that can inspire devotion. And from politics it's but a short hop to entertainment, where charisma is the indispensable handmaiden of anchorpersons, pitchpeople, and movie stars.

We like **gurgitate,** because it doesn't really exist in its own right — if it means anything, it means *to whirl* or *surge,* but it's really derived from *regurgitate,* which means *to whirl or surge <u>back,</u>* and is

Which is why she sends me out
Every morning before school
As a scout
To scour the neighborhood
In search of our beat-up, dented, rusty, secondhand
    automobile —
Which no one will steal —
And why every morning
Before the bus
There's this terrible fuss
When she looks at me in a kind of bleary miasma
And I have to tell her
All over again
Sunshine or rain
"I don't know where the CAR IS, MA."

---

used particularly of ruminant animals (like cows) that bring food *back* from their stomachs to their mouths and chew it all over again — **D*licious**! Believe it or not, this is exactly analogous to the process we've done here, which is to form a word backward from an existing word, so that it looks as though it's the original. This process, in linguistics, is called *back formation*.

    We'll leave **Phenomenon, Denizen,** and **Miasma** (sounds like a law firm) to your own detective agency. But we'd like to take you for a short ride on the **bus.** *Bus* is an abbreviation for (or a back formation from) *omnibus,* which is what all buses were originally called, and which is Latin for *to, for, by, with,* or *from everybody.* And so it is — the great democratic form of transportation.

LEARNING TO DRIVE

You drive me to distraction
You drive me round the bend
You drive me barmy, bonkers, bats, bananas
Will this driving never end?

You drive me to Darjeeling
You drive me up the wall
You drive me up a blooming tree —
Perhaps you better not drive at all.

How many words or phrases for *crazy* can you come up with? How many can you invent? We invented a paltry one — you could invent hundreds. Incidentally, why do so many words for *crazy* start with the letter *b*? (**Alliteration,** Megan — **whoopee!**)

PROFESSIONAL ASPIRATIONS

PHAR*MA*CIST

If I became a pharmacist
No one would come to harm
Because I know what fun it is
To help out on a pharm.

SOR*CER*ER'S AP*PREN*TICE

I want to be a sorcerer's apprentice
When I finally grow up
I'd love to learn to make a sorcer
And even the occasional plate or cup.

CHILD PSY*CHOL*OL*OGIST

When I grow up I want to be
A child psychol*
                    ologist
Because, of all my loves and likes,
The thing I like best is to fix kids' bikes.

If you trace **pharmacist** and **sorcerer** back to their roots (in Greek and French), you will discover that both of them have to do with witchcraft. Interesting, no? The wife of one and mother of two of us is in her professional life a child psychologist, so we will refrain from drawing any further parallels.

AG*O*RA*PHO*BI*A

Agoraphobia
Is a very long word
Spell it:
I-T

This is one of the oldest jokes in the universe. We heard it originally about **Constantinople.** In **Istanbul,** which is what Constantinople is called today, they're probably still using Constantinople. And in Constantinople they were probably using **Byzantium,** which is what Constantinople was called, even before it became the head (or seat — isn't language wonderful?) of the Roman Empire in A.D. 330. We happen to like the sound of *agoraphobia.* You can substitute any long word or name you like — how about **Zbigniew Brzezinski**?

    Agoraphobia, by the way, comes from (where else?) the Greek. *Agora* means *marketplace,* and *phobia* means *fear:* so, literally, fear of the marketplace, or, more generally, fear of crowds and open spaces; the exact opposite of *claustrophobia,* fear of enclosed spaces. Neither of these should be confused with *angoraphobia,* fear of longhaired cats and sweaters.

IT

IT
is nothing

IT
is a tiny
minuscule
insignificant word

With the exception of
A
I
and O!
as tiny and insignificant
as it gets

And yet
But
However
Notwithstanding
Moreover
Thereunto
In addition
Nevertheless
Verily, verily,
I say unto you . . .

All this **Verily, verily, I say unto you** stuff is taken directly from the King James Version of the Bible, the so-called Authorized Version, an English translation from the Greek and Hebrew that came out in 1611, and that, together with Shakespeare (who died in 1616), created the glorious, rich foundation for Modern English.

Have you seen the sun set
over the Shalimar?
(Or even the Jersey Turnpike?)
Can you describe
it?

Have you seen the Sistine Chapel
with the hand of God reaching out to Adam?
(Or replays of Willie Mays
    with his outstretched arm
    making The Catch?)
Can you depict
it?

Have you heard
the last great thunderous symphony
of Ludwig van Beethoven?
(Or a summer storm
    dumping hats full of rain
    on a tin roof
    in the dead of night
    with you awake in your bed below
    and only that shuddering sliver of tin
    between you and the almighty heavens?)
Can you repeat
it?

We stole **hats full of rain** from the title of a play by Michael V. Gazzo, an actor, writer, and member of the famous Actors Studio in New York (you can see him in *The Godfather*). It's always a good idea to acknowledge literary theft (the polite word is *allusion*), otherwise you may be accused of plagiarism — but then all work and no plagiarism is no fun at all.

Not easy, huh?
Even one.
And there are billions

Yup.
All those its
(Not to mention those zits)
and their brothers and sisters
make quite a collection

So
you see
IT
can be
the sun, the moon, the stars
the most wonderful and unimaginable
things
heaven and earth
the entire universe
agoraphobia
(or even a zit)

Yes, Horatio
there is more to IT
than is dreamt of
in your philosophy

IT
is everything.

If you're wondering who **Horatio** is and why he makes an appearance here, you need to go back to *Hamlet,* specifically Act I, Scene v, where Hamlet sees the ghost of his father and his buddy Horatio happens along. . . . We are of course borrowing here (or alluding), *not* plagiarizing. And if it seems like a misquotation, it is of course a deliberate misquotation. . . .

AH, ART

Art is that
About which when
As at the doctor for a throat
You should pardon the expression
Culture
In the presence of
Opening
You say
Either in stupefaction
Or in awe
Ah

This poem looks like **gibberish,** right? (Nice word, by the way, *gibberish.*) However, if you work at it a bit, hack your way through the thickets of main clauses and subordinate clauses (not to mention the thinnets), you may discover that what it has to say is actually exceedingly simple, though, we humbly submit, as our last word on the subject, not stupid. **Ridiculous,** maybe, but *not* **stupid.**

GLOSSING AND FLOSSING

Despite all our talk of filling your house with dictionaries, we decided, after much thought and arm wrestling, to include a **glossary.** A glossary is a miniature **dictionary.** The two words have similar origins. *Dictionary* comes, via French, from the Latin word for *speaking. Glossary* comes from the Greek word *glossa,* meaning *tongue,* which is of course *how* we speak. Incidentally, from the French word for *tongue, langue,* we get *language.* Tracing the history of words in this way is called *etymology* — one of the great tools of the literary detective — and it shows you how connected everything is — **tongue, language, speech** — and how we as humans, in different cultures and at different times, have developed along similar, often identical, lines.

    Gloss in this sense shouldn't be confused with its homonym (remember our old friend homonym?), *gloss,* which means *shine,* and which comes not from the Greek, but from the Old Norse and Icelandic — you can put those dictionaries away now. Actually, on second thought, hold on to them. Our little glossary will give you the barest of bones, perhaps enough to help you out if you're stuck. For the real detective work — which is where it becomes fun — you will need more than a glossary, you will need a . . . (or two or three or eight).

    And, remember, regular glossing and flossing gets you nice **shiny words** you can really sink your teeth into.

Acrostic — the initial letters of lines in a poem that if read in sequence form a word or phrase: A Careful Reading Of Some Texts Is Critical

Adieu — French for *Good-bye* — literally, [I commend you] *to God,* as in the Spanish *Adios* (or, for that matter, the English *Good-bye,* which is a contraction of *God be with you*)

Agoraphobia — fear of open spaces

Alliteration — the rich, rolling, and regular repetition of two or more initial consonants in neighboring words, also called **head rhyme** or **initial rhyme**

Analogous — comparable

Ancillary — supplementary

Apostrophe — 1. a mark to indicate the omission of a letter. 2. an address to someone usually absent (or o'itted)

Belatedly — past the normal time, as in "Don't you think you're going to bed a bit belatedly?" (Hey, alliteration!)

Boue — French for *mud*

Charisma — grace, beauty, kindness, compelling radiance

Clerihew — named for Edmund Clerihew Bentley, who wrote hundreds of these four-line poems

Coup — from the French for *hit* or *blow,* usually used in a political sense to indicate a hit or blow at the government (generally resulting in an *overthrow*)

Denizen — inhabitant

Depredation — plundering, from the same root (in Latin via French) as *prey* and *apprehend*

Diminutive — tiny; an affectionate shortening of a name

Envoi — the traditional poet's farewell to his book

Eponymous — relating to the person for whom something is named (there's that *nym* again)

Etymology — science of the derivation of words

Exhort — to encourage

Gibberish — unintelligible rubbish — the etymology for this seems to be entirely *onomatopoeic*

Homograph — having the same spelling

Homonym — having the same name

Homophone — having the same sound

Hue — 1. tint 2. cry, as in *hue and cry*

Illustrious — brilliantly outstanding; related, as *illustrator,* to *lustre*

Levitate — to (cause to) rise or float in the air, from the Latin for *light,* and thus the exact opposite of *gravitate,* as *levity* is of *gravity*

Limerick — somehow related to Limerick in Ireland (perhaps by Irish soldiers bringing this verse form back from France in the early 18th century)

Miasma — from the Greek for *pollution;* noxious fumes

Ministration — aid or service, related to *minister*

Moniker — a nickname or alias, used by hobos in the early 20th century — then by criminals

Onomatopoeia — the naming of a thing by imitating the sound associated with it

Oxymoron — a contradiction of words, as in *jumbo shrimp*

Palindrome — a word or sentence reading the same backward as forward

Paraphernalia — miscellaneous articles, trappings

Phenomenon — a rare and significant event or appearance, from the Greek for *appear*

Philologist — a lover of language

Plagiarism — stealing someone else's words, thoughts, ideas — from a Latin root for *kidnap*

Poetic License — something you can get away with in a poem (or similar) that you couldn't get away with in real life

Poietes — The Greek word for *poet*

Proboscis — an elephant's trunk

Prosaic — the prose equivalent of *poetic;* ordinary

Queue — the British word for *line* (not what you draw or what you fish with, but the kind you're in at lunch or at a bus stop); originally the French word for *tail*

Rebuttal — a contradictory argument, from the French meaning *to push back*

Roux — a sauce made from heating flour and fat

Ruminate — literally, to chew the cud; by extension, to reflect or ponder

Simile — a comparison of one thing with another

Sonnet — a verse form of fourteen lines, originally Italian

Transmogrify — to transform completely — from a completely bogus nonexistent Latin root!

Vernacular — common or informal (as opposed to literary or formal) language — e.g., English as opposed to Latin, Yiddish as opposed to Hebrew

Villanelle — a verse form (originally French) of five three-line stanzas and one four-liner. Check out Dylan Thomas's "Do Not Go Gentle into That Good Night" or Edward Arlington Robinson's "House on the Hill."

Weltschmerz — from the German, literally *world pain,* i.e., the kind of pain you get when you compare the actual miserable state of the world with your ideal of what it should be

Widget — useless or unnecessary gadget or frill

ENVOI

To Annie, Archie, Bob, and Chris
Our thanks and many a heartfelt kiss.
To Gertie, Georges, Francesco, Frank
Our kisses and many a heartfelt thank.
To Dylan, Ed, Mike, Tom, and Will
We love you then, now, all, and still.

We gaze on you in admiration
We doff our hat and crook a leg
We crave your kind consideration
For the humble *poi*e*tes* of FEG.